Romans

STUDIES IN THIS SERIES

Available from Marshall Morgan & Scott

How to Start a Small Group Bible Study A Guide to Discussion Study

Mark: Examine the Record (recommended as first unit of study)

The Acts of the Apostles

Romans

Four Men of God Abraham, Joseph, Moses, David

ROMANS

16 Discussions for Group Bible Study

Marilyn Kunz and
Catherine Schell

small group bible studies

Marshalls

Marshalls Paperbacks
Marshall Morgan & Scott
3 Beggarwood Lane, Basingstoke, Hants, RG23 7LP, UK

British Library CIP data
Schell, Catherine
    Romans.——(Small group Bible studies)
    1. Bible. N.T. Romans——Commentaries
    I. Title   II. Kunz, Marilyn   III. Series
    227'.106   BS2665.3

    ISBN 0 – 551 – 01202 – 1

Printed in Great Britain by Stanley L. Hunt (Printers) Ltd. Rushden,
Northamptonshire.

Contents

How to Use
This Discussion Guide

HOW TO PREPARE TO LEAD A STUDY

(1) Pray for wisdom and the Holy Spirit's guidance.
(2) Read the Bible passage through, thoughtfully, at least twice.
(3) Study the discussion questions and think through the answers as you find them in the passage.
(4) Look over the questions again, and think through how you will rephrase them into your own words. This will help your leadership of the discussion to be truly your own.
(5) Pray for the ability to guide the discussion with love and understanding.

HOW TO LEAD A STUDY

(1) Begin with prayer for minds open to understand, and hearts willing to obey, the Word of the Lord. You may ask another member of the group to pray if you have asked him ahead of time.
(2) Have the passage read aloud by sections.
(3) Guide the group to discover what the passage says by asking the questions which you have prepared.
(4) Consider together the summary questions for the study, and encourage each one to be honest in self-appraisal. You must take the lead in spiritual honesty. Avoid hypocrisy in any form.
(5) Bring the discussion to a close at the end of the time allotted, summarizing the impact that this passage can have upon your situation today. You as leader or one of the group members may summarize.
(6) Close in a prayer of thanksgiving or committal.

HOW TO ENCOURAGE EVERYONE TO PARTICIPATE

(1) Encourage discussion by asking several people to contribute answers to a question. "What do the rest of you think?" or "Is there anything else which could be added?" are ways of encouraging discussion.

(2) Be flexible and skip any questions which do not fit into the discussion as it progresses.

(3) Deal with irrelevant issues by suggesting that the purpose of your study is to discover what is *in the passage*. Suggest an informal chat about tangential or controversial issues after the regular study is dismissed.

(4) Receive all contributions warmly. Never bluntly reject what anyone says, even if you think the answer is incorrect. Instead ask in a friendly manner, "Where did you find that?" or "Is that actually what it says?" or "What do some of the rest of you think?" Allow the group to handle problems together.

(5) Be sure you don't talk too much as the leader. Redirect those questions which are asked you. A discussion should move in the form of an asterisk, back and forth between members, not in the form of a fan, with the discussion always coming back to the leader. The leader is to act as moderator. As members of a group get to know each other better, the discussion will move more freely, progressing from the fan to the asterisk patttern.

(6) Don't be afraid of pauses or long silences. People need time to think about the questions and the passage. Never, *never* answer your own question—either use an alternate question or move on to another area for discussion.

(7) Watch hesitant members for an indication by facial expression or bodily posture that they have something to say, and then give them an encouraging nod or speak their names.

(8) Discourage too talkative members from monopolizing the discussion by specifically directing questions to others. If necessary speak privately to the over-talkative one about the need for discussion rather than lecture in the group, and enlist his aid in encouraging all to participate.

Introduction to the Letter to the Romans

The letter to the Romans, written by the Apostle Paul from Corinth, is dated between 56 and 59 A.D. It is most generally believed to have been written about 58 A.D. during Paul's three-month stay at Corinth on his third missionary journey, shortly before his return to Jerusalem as described in Acts 20:3. This letter to a church he had not founded or indeed ever visited was written in connection with a proposed visit he hoped to make to Rome. (See Acts 19:21; 23:11.) It was three years later that Paul did visit Rome as a prisoner. Perhaps it was his desire to introduce himself to these Christians and also his awareness that his days were numbered (Acts 20:22, 23, 37, 38) which caused Paul to write in this letter a detailed explanation of the gospel of God in Jesus Christ.

The church at Rome probably dated from the time when Jews from Rome were in Jerusalem on the day of Pentecost (Acts 2:10) and witnessed the outpouring of the Holy Spirit. Some of these Roman Jews were no doubt among the five thousand added that day to the church of Jesus Christ (Acts 2:41). Rome was the center of the civilized world and the church there was made up of both Jews and Gentiles. There seems to have been no central organization of the church at Rome, but there were at least four congregations which met in various homes. One of these congregations met, it is believed, at the home of Priscilla and Aquila, who are the first to whom Paul sends greetings at the close of his letter in Romans 16:3. These two whom Paul first met at Corinth were evidently already Christians from Rome; they accompanied Paul on part of his second missionary journey and were influential in the church at Ephesus (Acts 18:1, 2, 18, 19, 24–28).

The significance of this letter cannot be overstated. It is undoubtedly the most important letter in the history of mankind, and volumes have been written about it. However, the true influence of this letter must be measured not by the words written about it but by the lives which have been transformed by reading it. Within ten years of receiving this letter, the church at Rome became the object of severe persecution by the Emperor who made the Christians his scapegoat for the fire of Rome, 64 A.D. From what we know of the steadfastness of the Christians' faith at that time, we can be assured that this letter to the Romans bore fruit from the beginning.

Why Is Salvation Necessary?

From the very outset of this letter, Paul begins to deal with the basic issues of the Christian faith. He sets forth the reasons for the alienation which exists between God and man.

Romans 1:1–7

(1) From this paragraph, what do you learn about the author and the recipients of this letter?

(2) What do you learn about the origin of the gospel? about any prior prediction of the gospel? about the subject or content of the gospel?

(3) What do you learn about Jesus Christ?

Romans 1:8–15

(4) What seems to be Paul's purpose in writing to the Christians at Rome? (Include verses 5, 6.) What kind of relationship does he establish with those to whom he is writing? How? What things does Paul specifically claim?

Romans 1:16, 17

(5) What is revealed here about the power of the gospel? Keep in mind what Paul has already stated about the gospel in the first paragraph and in verse 15.

(6) In verses 16, 17 Paul states the theme of his letter. Put this theme into your own words.

(7) Why should Paul find it necessary to proclaim that he is not ashamed of the gospel? (See I Corinthians 1:22, 23.)

(8) What connection does faith have with salvation and with righteousness? For whom is salvation available?

Note—Verse 17, "the righteousness of God" here refers to God's provision of righteousness for man in Christ.

Romans 1:18–23

(9) What exactly is man's sin against which God's wrath is revealed? What choices did man have open to him? What choice has he made?

(10) Why are men without excuse? What two things ought men to have done?

(11) What have been the consequences of sin in man's intellect and in his spiritual life?

(12) From this paragraph, what opportunity is given to every human being, even to those in primitive societies?

Romans 1:24–32

(13) How is God's wrath (verse 18) expressed in His actions in verses 24, 26, 28 and in His decree in verse 32? What does this indicate about the nature of God's punishment? How is it a punishment for man to be allowed to have his own way?

(14) How does Paul restate man's basic sin in verse 25? What were the results when God gave men up? (Verses 24, 26–31)

(15) From what do all these sins stem? Why is there no indication of degrees of sin? Under what penalty do all sins fall?

(16) How does moral degradation reach its depths in verse 32?

SUMMARY

(1) Describe the state of the Gentiles as pointed out in this passage. Why are men in this condition?

(2) In what ways do we as individuals and as a nation fail to comply with the demands of verses 21, 25, 28?

(3) In the light of this chapter, what is my spiritual situation?

CONCLUSION

Man's basic problem is in his relationship with God, theological rather than moral. His alienation from God stems from his rejection of God. Man is therefore under a death sentence and he will die if he is not rescued. The gospel is the way of rescue, and contains the power to deliver any man from the desperate predicament in which he finds himself.

What About the Jew?

In case his Jewish readers should think themselves immune from the condemnation described in the first chapter, Paul here clarifies the position of the Jew in relation to God.

Romans 2:1–16

(1) To whom is this section addressed? What does Paul accuse them of doing? To what do "the very same things" (verse 1) and "such things" (verses 2, 3) refer? See Romans 1:32, then 1:28–31.

(2) What is Paul trying to make clear by the questions he asks in verses 3, 4? What is the result of a hard and impenitent heart (verse 5)? Consider the terrible contrast between the "riches" in verse 4 and what is "treasured up" or "stored up" in verse 5.

(3) List the characteristics and the results of God's judgment as described in verses 5–11. Note the words "seek" (verse 7) and "obey" (verse 8). Behind the works of each man, what does God see?

(4) Remember that the Jew possessed the written law (the revealed will of God) in the Old Testament Scriptures. The non-Jew (Gentile) did not have the written law. According to verses 12–16, what will be the basis of God's judgment in relation to the law? Why are not all Jews automatically declared righteous (justified) before God?

(5) In what ways does God's judgment (verses 11, 16) differ from man's judgment? How does it differ from the judgment given by the man in verse 1?

Romans 2:17–29

(6) The Jews prided themselves on the law (verse 17) and circumcision (verse 25). What claims of the Jew does Paul outline in verses 17–20?

(7) What indictment does Paul bring against the Jew in verses 21–24?

(8) How have the actions of the Jew reflected upon God? Why? (Verse 24)

(9) If Paul were addressing verses 17–24 today to the Christian church, what changes or additions might he make? How are his accusations applicable to us as Christians?

(10) In verses 25–29, how does Paul deal with that in which the Jew put his supreme confidence? For the significance of circumcision, read Genesis 17:1–14.

(11) Upon what does the value of outward religious performance such as circumcision depend? See also Deuteronomy 10:16.

(12) In verses 17–29, how does Paul strip the Jews of their pride and sense of superiority over the Gentiles? Whom does God praise?

SUMMARY

(1) Summarize the nature and condition of all men, Jew and Gentile, as set forth in the first two chapters of Romans.

(2) Why is self-righteousness, whatever form it takes, of no value?

CONCLUSION

All men are judged by God, not on what they say but on what they do, not on outward conformity such as circumcision, but on the inner motive of the heart. Man's heart and his spiritual state determine his relationship with God.

What Hope Is There?

Paul realizes that the statements he has made thus far in his letter will raise a number of questions. He deals briefly with these questions in verses 1–18, and then presents the core of the whole letter—justification and its consequences.

Romans 3:1–8

(1) Try to find each objection (verses 1, 3, 5, 7, 8) which Paul can see being raised as a result of his condemnation of Jewish "righteousness" in chapter 2.

(2) What brief answer does Paul give to each objection? To what attributes of God does he hold fast? Note—Verse 2, "oracles of God"—the law of God given at Mount Sinai and the word of God given through the prophets.

Romans 3:9–18

(3) What is Paul's contention concerning all men including the Jews? How does he substantiate his statement? Note—Verses 10–18 are Old Testament quotations, most of them from the Psalms, which represent the law and describe the Jews in particular.

(4) Think carefully about each word picture drawn in verses 11–18. What do these Old Testament quotations point out about man's thoughts, man's direction, man's speech, and man's pursuits?

(5) What do verses 11 and 18 indicate concerning the basic problem of man? Compare with 1:28.

Romans 3:19, 20

(6) Verses 19, 20 serve as a summary of chapters 1 and 2. What conclusion does Paul draw from his previous reasoning in chapters 1 and 2, and from the Old Testament passages just quoted?

(7) How inclusive is the statement in verse 19b? The reason for the inclusiveness of this statement is given in verse 20. What pathway for justification before God has been blocked?

(8) What function *does* the law have, according to verse 20?

(9) Why is it impossible for man by his own efforts to escape the condemnation of God's judgment?

Romans 3:21-26

Note—This is one of the most important sections in the New Testament and should be carefully considered by the group until each one understands its meaning.

(10) In verses 21, 22 "the righteousness of God" does not concern His character, but is best understood according to Williams' translation—"God's way of giving men right standing with Himself," or Today's English Version—"God's way of putting men right with Himself." How has Paul prepared his readers to consider God's way of righteousness by what he has already shown about Gentile righteousness and Jewish righteousness? See also verses 22b, 23.

(11) In verses 21-26 discover as many distinct points as you can which are made about God's way of righteousness, this way of salvation. Make a list of these points.

(12) What are the terms or conditions of this salvation? To whom do they apply? Why?

(13) How is justification described in verses 24, 25? How is it brought about? Note—"Justify" is to count as righteous, to pronounce righteous. "Redemption" is release or deliverance effected by payment of a ransom. "Propitiation" or "expiation" is not the placating or conciliating of an angry God by sinful humanity, but it is the full satisfaction of the demands of God's righteous law against sinful man by the death of God's own Son.

(14) What is the importance of faith in God's way of righteousness? What or who is the object of faith?

Romans 3:27-31

(15) What are the consequences of this gift of righteousness? Why has man no longer any cause for self pride?

(16) In verses 29, 30, what facts are stated about God? about justification?

(17) What is the answer to man's sinful condition?

(18) What ways of righteousness do people attempt? Why are these ways futile?

CONCLUSION

As Jew and Gentile both stand condemned and without excuse before God by their failure to keep the law they possess, both are eligible through faith in Christ for God's free gift of right standing with Himself. God looks beyond their external circumcision or lack of it to see their faith in His Son whose death on the cross delivered men from the bondage of sin and from the righteous wrath of God. The grace of God (His undeserved love toward sinners) eliminates any possible reason for any man to boast before Him.

This page may be used for study notes.

What About Those Who Lived During the Old Testament Era?

Abraham is an example of how faith operates in a man's life to bring him into right relationship with God.

Romans 4:1–12

(1) In verses 1–8, what instances from the Old Testament does Paul use to substantiate his point that justification (God's way of giving men right standing before Him) comes by faith and not by works?

(2) How did Abraham achieve right standing or righteousness? How did David achieve it?

(3) Was Abraham reckoned righteous before or after he was circumcised? What was the significance of circumcision in his life?

(4) Who then are the children of Abraham? How would an understanding of the teaching in verses 11, 12 affect the controversy in the early church over the admission of the Gentiles who believed in Christ (described in Acts 15)?

Romans 4:13–25

(5) Abraham's faith was focused on a particular promise. What does Paul say about this promise (verses 13–16)? To whom was it made? It came through what? On what does it depend? Why?

(6) What is the tense of the verb in the promise quoted in verse 17? Why is this significant? When was the promise made to Abraham? See also Genesis 15:1–6.

(7) In verses 18–21, how did Abraham respond to the promise? What facts of his situation would have tended to make him doubt?

(8) Pick out the verbs in verses 18–21 which describe Abraham's reactions. What indicates the degree of his faith?

(9) How does Abraham compare with Thomas in John 20:24–29?

(10) Why did Abraham believe this promise which, from a human viewpoint, was outrageous? What was the result for Abraham?

(11) God's dealings with Abraham are recorded for our benefit (verses 23, 24). How is God described in verses 17b and 24? Compare what Abraham believed about God with what we must believe about God if we are to be counted righteous (Romans 4:23–25; Genesis 15:4–6; Hebrews 11:11, 12, 17–19).

(12) What was the purpose of Jesus' death and resurrection? In what sense were our sins the cause of Jesus' death? Compare verse 25 with I Peter 2:24 and Isaiah 53:5, 6, 8b, 11.

SUMMARY

(1) Just as many people do today, the Jews in Paul's time believed that their works would justify them before a holy God. How does Paul correct this erroneous idea?

(2) The essence of salvation for men through all ages has been that they must not only believe in God, but they must believe God. For Abraham that included all that God said in His promise to him. For us it includes all that God has said in Jesus Christ. From your studies thus far in Romans, how would you explain to someone else exactly what faith in Jesus Christ means?

CONCLUSION

Abraham, the father of the Jewish nation, and David, their greatest king, were both men who obtained right standing before God by faith apart from works. In fact, Abraham's circumcision was a sign of the acceptance he had with God by faith before he was circumcised. God wants men today to be like Abraham, to believe Him when He speaks, to accept His promise by faith, to believe in Him as the One who raised Jesus from the dead. When a man does this, he has right standing before God.

What Are the Results for Us of Justification by Faith?

Paul explains how Jesus Christ is the agent of our justification, the channel of life for the one who believes.

Romans 5:1–11

(1) What things are ours through our Lord Jesus Christ? by His blood? by His death? by His life? (Verses 1, 2, 9–11). What must we do to receive these benefits (4:24)?

Note—Verse 2, "access" means introduction into the presence of God, favor with God.

(2) What are the three things in which we may now rejoice (verses 2, 3, 11)? Why may even suffering now be viewed differently?

(3) In what specific way did God manifest His love? Note the extent of God's love in comparison to man's love.

(4) What words in verses 6, 8, 10 describe our former condition? What is the significance of each description? How did God's love manifested meet each aspect of our condition?

(5) How secure is the future for the Christian, as described by the two "much more" statements in verses 9, 10?

(6) What does the word "reconciliation" indicate about a relationship? How are our reconciliation with God and our enjoyment of it accomplished?

Romans 5:12–21

(7) What facts do you learn about sin and death from verses 12–14? Which came first? What were the effects? Why do men die?

(8) Note—In this section Adam and Christ ("the one who was to come"—verse 14) are compared. Each was a man who represented the human race, a man whose acts brought vast consequences to all mankind because of the solidarity (unity) of the human race.

Verses 15–17 list a series of contrasts between the trespass of Adam and the free gift of God. What is the free gift? What are these contrasts? What are the results of the trespass of Adam and the gift of Christ? (See verses 18, 19.)

(9) What effect did the law have? Compare verse 20 with verse 13.

(10) In what ways is grace more than a match for sin? What are the consequences of grace and of sin?

(11) How do we obtain eternal life? Note 5: 17; 6: 23.

SUMMARY

What is the connection between the death of Christ and our justification before God?

CONCLUSION

Paul describes the experience of salvation he shares with his fellow Christian believers. He outlines the magnitude of God's grace as revealed in His gift of righteousness in Jesus Christ. Only by receiving God's gift of righteousness through Jesus Christ can a man escape condemnation and death, and enjoy eternal life.

Why Do Good if Justification Comes by Faith Alone?

For fear that some should think that God's grace is an occasion for man to be irresponsible, Paul now deals with the question of sin and the believer. In this chapter he regards sin as a tyrant master holding men in bondage.

Romans 6:1–14

(1) How does Paul answer the objection that justification *by faith alone* encourages people to sin as much as they like because sinning gives the grace of God a chance to operate? What is the purpose of salvation as far as sin is concerned?

(2) About whom is Paul talking in verses 3, 4? What does baptism symbolize?

(3) In verses 4–8, what are the experiences and the results of the believer's union with Christ? What condition does the word "if" (verses 5, 8) put upon the outcome? How important is the cross? See also 3:23–25 and 5:10.

(4) What does the Christian know (verses 9–11), and what must he do with this knowledge? What is the first step for the Christian in attaining victory over sin?

(5) What must the Christian do to live a life consistent with his position before God in Christ Jesus? What must he not do? (Verses 12–14).

(6) What does living "under grace" mean as against living "under the law"? What is the consequence for the Christian (verse 14)?

Romans 6:15–23

(7) Lest anyone think that living under grace gives one the liberty to commit sin, what reminder does Paul give concerning our choices?

(8) In this section "servant" is rightly translated "slave." List the contrasts drawn in verses 16–19.

(9) Between what two masters must a man choose (verse 16)? What information does Paul give which would help in making this choice?

(10) What command is so important that Paul repeats it (verses 13, 19)? From the expressions "for as...so now..." (verse 19), what do you learn about how to serve God?

(11) Verses 20–22 continue the contrasts drawn between the former and the present state of these Christians. What is the present result and the final conclusion of their present way of life?

(12) What is holiness or sanctification (verse 22)? Does verse 22 suggest that sanctification earns us eternal life? How does verse 23 clarify any misconception? How *do* we get eternal life?

SUMMARY

(1) The previous chapters have shown that Christ's righteousness reckoned *for* us brings us into a position of *justification* or right standing with God. Chapter 6 points out that as we who are justified by faith are obedient to God, He works Christ's righteousness *in* us, the experience of *sanctification*. How has chapter 6 argued for the necessity of "walking in newness of life"?

(2) From this study, what would you tell someone who wants to know what is required to live a "holy" life?

CONCLUSION

The Christian has been freed not only from the penalty of sin but also from the ruling power of sin through Jesus Christ. No longer slaves to sin which dominated us, now free to choose our master, we must now submit ourselves to God's reign of righteousness in our lives.

How Can I Please God?

The issue here is the Christian's relationship to the law as in the previous chapter the issue was the Christian's relationship to sin.

Romans 7:1–6

(1) How is it possible to be set free from subjection to the law? Put into your own words the illustration of this given in verses 2, 3. How is this principle applied in verse 4?

(2) What new relationship is established? What is the "fruit" of the old union? What is the "fruit" of the new union?

Note—Instead of being subject to the law and having to keep a list of rules and regulations, the person who has died and risen with Christ is married to Christ and is motivated to do His will out of love.

(3) How does the death mentioned in verse 4 deliver us from the power of sin? Compare 6:6, 7 and 7:5, 6.

Note—"In the flesh" means according to our human nature apart from God and unaided by God. The flesh means all that man is without God and without Christ.

Romans 7:7–13

(4) List the specific things Paul says about the law in this section.

(5) What is the purpose of the law? What did the law reveal in Paul's own life?

(6) What statements are made concerning sin and its effects? What was its result as far as Paul was concerned?

(7) What does verse 13 conclude about sin?

(8) What discovery has the law helped Paul to make about himself?

Romans 7:14–25

(9) What does this section show to be the stronger force in a man's life—the external law or indwelling sin? Inevitably then, what is the result of life "under the law"?

(10) What contrast does Paul make between the law and himself (verse 14)? Why would this work against his keeping the law?

(11) How does Paul describe the battle within? What happens when Paul wants to do right and to please God?

(12) Count the number of "I's" in verses 14–23. What significance does this give to verse 24? Why is it meaningful that he says "who" and not "how" in verse 24?

(13) Man needs deliverance from the condemnation pronounced by the law of God, and he needs a power within greater than the power of sin so that he can do God's will. How are both needs provided in Jesus Christ our Lord (verse 25a)?

SUMMARY

How does this chapter show that we cannot live holy lives by our own strength any more than we can attain right standing before God by our own works?

CONCLUSION

Union with Christ in his death sets a man free from subjection to the law, while union with Christ in His resurrection brings a man into the new life of the Spirit. Thus the complete dependence of the Christian on the Lord Jesus Christ is emphasized in this chapter. Even in attempts at positive righteousness the Christian is helpless in his own strength and will.

What Is the Christian Life?

The full solution to the problems outlined in chapters 6 and 7 is given in this chapter. The how and why of daily Christian living is here described.

Romans 8:1–17

(1) How does Paul sum up his letter thus far in verse 1? State this verse in a positive form rather than as a negative summary. What relationship is essential?

(2) In verses 2–4, what reasons does Paul give for his confidence?

(3) What two ways of life are described in verses 4b–8? What things are true about each? How does the human mind operate in this situation? What are the results?

(4) What are the conditions ("if" statements) in verses 9–11? In each case, what kind of a relationship is suggested? What are the promises if these conditions are met? Which promises are present? Which promises are future?

(5) What evidences for the Trinity of God are found in verses 9–11?

(6) In verses 12–17, what further statements are made concerning the two ways of life? What are their results? What new things are revealed about the Christian life, the life according to the Spirit?

(7) What two aspects of the Christian life are suggested in verses 13, 14? How is the Christian empowered?

(8) What two spirits are contrasted in verse 15? How does Paul develop the full meaning of sonship? How does he again emphasize the importance of our relationship to Christ?

Romans 8:18–39

(9) What present conditions are described in verses 18–25? What things are awaited? By whom? What do Christians already possess? Why are Christians subject to suffering? Why is hope as well as faith part of the Christian life?

(10) What additional ministry does the Spirit perform (verses 26, 27)? What importance does this have for our praying as Christians?

(11) What is God's major purpose in the life of the Christian (verse 29)? How do the circumstances of verse 28 relate to this purpose? List the actions of God toward the believer (verse 30). How would understanding this purpose and these actions of God sustain the Christian through sufferings in this life?

(12) What Paul has said in verses 18–30 can help the Christian to *endure* suffering. In verses 31–39, what reasons does he give for *rejoicing* and *triumphing over* suffering? What specific evidences do we have of God's love?

(13) What does verse 34 indicate about the person and work of the Lord Jesus?

(14) What possible situations are suggested by verses 35–37? Give examples of such situations today over which the Christian may be victorious. How can the Christian conquer? What security does the Christian have?

(15) In what way do the claims in verses 38, 39 start where the previous series in verse 35 ends? What greater claims are made? In what does the Christian put absolute confidence?

SUMMARY

(1) What do you learn from this chapter about the Christian life?

(2) Give some practical examples of living like this in today's world.

CONCLUSION

The twofold secret of Christian living is described by two phrases in verses 1 and 10—"in Christ Jesus" and "if Christ is in you." The Christian for his part sets his will to live in Christ Jesus a life pleasing to God. The Lord for His part dwells in us empowering us to live such a life. The work of the Trinity on behalf of the Christian is outlined from verse 26 to the end of the chapter.

What About All the Promises God Made to the Jews?

At this point in his letter Paul has finished his proclamation of the doctrines of justification, sanctification, and glorification. All seems ready for the practical application of these doctrines to the daily life of the Christian believer. However, the question of the Jews emerges. The good news of salvation by faith in place of righteousness through law-keeping opens the door of salvation to the Gentiles, but it wipes out the covenant rights and privileges of the Jewish people and bypasses them as the channel for God's progressive revelation of Himself and His purposes.

The Jewish nation, God's chosen people, is neither being saved nor being of service to God. How can this be?

Romans 9:1-18

(1) After his great song of triumph at the conclusion of chapter 8, why does Paul still know sorrow and anguish? How deep is his concern for his fellow Jews?

(2) What great spiritual heritage does the Jew have? Define each part of that heritage mentioned in verses 4, 5. Concerning "the adoption" or "sonship" see Deuteronomy 14:1, 2; Exodus 4:22, 23. For "the glory" see Exodus 16:10; 24:16, 17. Concerning "covenants" see Genesis 9:12–17; 15:4–7, 3–16, 18.

(3) The fact that the Jews as a nation rejected the Christ raises the question, "Did the word of God fail? Did God fail to carry out His promises?" How does Paul answer this question in verses 6b–13?

(4) What is meant by "children of the flesh" (verse 8)? In this section, how are the flesh and works ruled ineffective as far as determining who are the people of God? When and why was Jacob chosen and Esau rejected to continue Abraham's line?

(5) Paul shows from Israel's history that not all physical descendants of Abraham were counted as the children of God but that God picked and chose the line of His people through Isaac, then through Jacob. Furthermore, this selection did not depend on human deeds or merit to earn it. What new question arises from this reasoning (verse 14)?

(6) How does God answer man's cry for justice? How is God's sovereignty expressed (verses 15–18)? Notice how Shakespeare expresses an understanding of this passage in the *Mer-*

chant of Venice (Act IV, Scene 1): "Therefore, Jew, though justice be thy plea, consider this, that, in the course of justice, none of us should see salvation: we do pray for mercy."

Romans 9:19–33

(7) In verses 20–23, what illustration from the village life of that day does Paul use?

(8) Express in your own words the question raised in verse 19. How is this question answered in verses 20, 21?

(9) In the two cases suggested in verses 22, 23, in which one has there been previous preparation? By whom? Who are included in the "vessels of mercy"? Who are the object of God's patience?

(10) Whom has God chosen, and for what (verses 23–29)?

(11) How does Paul prove from Old Testament Scriptures that God has called some of the Gentiles and only a portion of the Jews (verses 25, 26)?

(12) How then *can* righteousness be attained? Who succeeds in attaining it? Who fails? Why? Compare verses 32, 33 with James 2:10.

(13) What and who is the stumbling stone to Israel? Why? (Verses 30–33. See also I Corinthians 1:23.)

(14) What things had been foretold about this stone? What is the way of escape from stumbling and falling over this stone?

SUMMARY

(1) What does this chapter teach us about God?

(2) What does this chapter teach us about the Jews? about the Gentiles? Why should Israel's rejection of the Christ have been expected?

(3) What avenue to righteousness with God is open to Jew and Gentile?

CONCLUSION

Paul argues that God has *not* broken His promises. These promises are fulfilled to Abraham's spiritual children, the true Israel which includes both Jews and Gentiles who share Abraham's faith. God who is the Sovereign Creator has the right to show mercy to whom He will, including the Gentiles. Paul concludes that the basic problem of his people, the Jews, is their failure to recognize that righteousness is obtained through faith and not by works.

How Can the Jews Be Held Responsible for Their Unbelief?

Man's way of righteousness and God's way of righteousness are contrasted and the universal opportunity for salvation is described.

Romans 10:1–13

(1) About whom is Paul talking in verses 1–3? How does he feel about them? What virtue do they possess? Why have they failed? Compare with 9:31, 32.

(2) What contrasts are drawn between righteousness based on the law and righteousness based on faith? How is the way of salvation near and possible (verses 8–10)? What two elements are involved? Why are both necessary?

(3) What do verses 4 and 11 point out about Christ and salvation?

(4) How do verses 11–13 emphasize that the gospel has a universal application? What condition is repeated? State verse 13 in negative form.

(5) What in man's nature would tend to make him prefer righteousness based upon works rather than righteousness based upon faith? (Note the words "establish" and "submit" in verse 3.)

(6) What does it mean in this context (including verse 9) to call upon the name of the Lord? What three promises are made to the one who calls upon the Lord (verses 11, 12, 13)?

Romans 10:14–21

(7) Why can't the Jews find excuse by claiming as in verse 14 that they have had no opportunity or that they have had no warning? See verses 15b, 16, 18. Although the good news (the gospel) has been proclaimed, what has been the Jews' response?

(8) What responsibility is placed upon the one who hears the message of salvation through faith in Jesus Christ (verses 16, 17)? What are the only two possible responses?

(9) What warnings were clearly given to the Jews through Moses and through Isaiah (verses 19–21)? What do these warnings show about the faith of the Gentiles and the response of the Jews? How were these things being fulfilled in the days of Paul's ministry? See Acts 13: 42–52; 14: 1–7.

(10) What picture of the Lord is drawn in verse 21? What picture of Israel does it reveal? Why should Israel's apostasy be no surprise?

SUMMARY

(1) What is the message of the gospel that is open to all? What responsibility is upon all who hear? How do verses 9, 10 sum up the response necessary for salvation?

(2) What does God mean when He refers to people as disobedient and contrary? How can I express the opposite attitudes toward Him?

CONCLUSION

The Jews, attempting to earn righteousness before God by keeping the law, have failed to obtain it while the Gentiles who were not even seeking God have believed the good news of God's gift of righteousness in Jesus Christ. Whether a man is a Jew or a Gentile, his salvation depends upon nothing more or less than what he thinks and does about Jesus. Submission to God's way of righteousness by personal acknowledgement of Jesus as the risen Lord brings a man into right standing with God.

ROMANS 11

Why Is Anti-Semitism Unthinkable for the Christian?

Paul defines the relationship between Jew and Gentile, and more specifically, the relationship between the Christian and the Jew. He also explains the division among the Jews concerning the Christ.

Romans 11:1–24

(1) What conclusion is Paul afraid his readers might reach from reading chapters 9 and 10? What does Paul seek to prove by the illustrations from his own life and from Elijah's experience?

(2) What division has been made in Israel? What is the experience of each segment (verses 1–10)?

(3) How do the quotations in verses 8–10 describe the attitudes and experiences of the Jews from Paul's time to ours? Give any specific illustrations you think fulfill these Scriptures.

(4) In verses 7, 11, 12, what makes Paul confident that Israel's rejection of the Gospel is not unanimous, and is not permanent?

(5) What series of causes and effects is set in motion by the Jews' failure to accept Christ (verses 11–15)?

(6) What does Paul say about his own ministry?

(7) With what two pictures does Paul illustrate his optimism about the Jews in verse 16?

(8) What is the point of the picture developed in verses 17–24? How many branches were broken off? Why?

(9) Against what attitudes are the Gentile Christians warned? Why? What attitude does Paul encourage?

(10) What hope does Paul have for the Jews? See verses 23, 24. Upon what does this hope depend from them? from God?

Romans 11:25–36

(11) What secret purposes of God in history are now revealed? Compare verse 25 with Mark 13:10 and Luke 21:23b, 24.

(12) Scholars differ as to whether "all Israel" (verse 26) means the true spiritual Israel which includes Jews and Gentiles,

33

or the Jews taken as a race. In either case, what future changes are predicted in verses 26, 27?

(13) What dual position do the Jews have at the present time (verse 28)? Why are they still beloved?

(14) What attitude toward God has been true of both Jews and Gentiles (verses 30, 31)? What is God's purpose toward each group?

(15) Why is the recognition of universal guilt, described in chapters 1–3 and restated in verse 32, necessary in God's plan in history?

(16) Compare verse 32 with 10:12, 13 to understand the conditions which put this mercy into effect.

(17) Having considered from the beginning of this letter man's condition and God's righteous, merciful dealings with man, Paul bursts forth into praise in verses 33–36. By what truths is the apostle overwhelmed?

(18) Compare the reminder in verses 34, 35 with 9:20.

SUMMARY

(1) In the light of this whole chapter, and especially verse 36, how are all men encompassed by God's plan in history through our Lord Jesus Christ?

(2) From all you have learned in chapters 9–11 about the debt the Christian owes to the Jew, what attitude should you as a Christian have toward Jews who have not recognized Jesus as the Christ (Messiah)?

CONCLUSION

The degree and extent of God's mercy is illustrated by His dealings with both Jew and Gentile. The interdependence of Jew and Gentile in God's plans and purposes removes from the Christian of Gentile background any reason for an attitude of pride or superiority toward the Jew. Humility and awe are the proper attitudes for both Gentile and Jew who experience the kindness of God.

What Should Characterize
the Life of the Christian?

Having shown how a man can get right and keep right with God, Paul proceeds to describe how such a man ought to live his daily life. He deals with the Christian's relationship to God, to his own self, to fellow Christians, and to all men.

Romans 12:1–8

(1) What appeal does Paul make in the light of all that he has said thus far in his letter? What are the "mercies of God" to which Paul refers? (Summarize briefly from chapters 3–11.)

(2) How do the "living sacrifice" and "spiritual worship" (or "reasonable service") of the Christian (verse 1) differ from the Old Testament sacrifices? Compare I Peter 2:5; Hebrews 13:15, 16.

(3) From verses 1, 2, what is the Christian's responsibility for his body and his mind? For a man to live a life acceptable to God, what must become the motivating center of his life? Compare with 8:5–7.

(4) What two possible outlooks on life are contrasted in verse 2?

(5) In verse 3, what practical suggestion does the apostle make concerning the use of the mind?

(6) Why is self-centeredness ruled out of the Christian life (verses 4, 5)? What do the particular functions or gifts mentioned in verses 6–8 indicate about the Christian life? Why is simply *having* these gifts not enough?

(7) What have the "grace" and "faith" in verses 3 and 6 to do with how the Christian is able to carry out the will of God?

(8) What attitudes should a Christian have toward God, toward the world, toward himself, toward his fellow Christians?

Romans 12:9–21

(9) What struggles in the Christian life are suggested by the three imperatives in verse 9? Why are each of these three commands basic to the Christian life?

(10) How do verses 10 and 13 expand upon verse 5? Describe the qualities of such a Christian fellowship. Give some

practical examples of this type of fellowship in action.

(11) Put into your own words the commands in verses 11, 12.

(12) Suggest words or phrases which sum up the Christian's attitude toward his fellow Christians (verses 10, 13) and his attitude toward the Lord (verses 11, 12).

(13) What difficult situations are mentioned in verses 14–21? How must each of these situations be met? What wrong attitudes and actions are forbidden?

(14) How does verse 21 sum up the dual task of the Christian in the world?

SUMMARY

(1) List briefly the positive commands to the Christian in this chapter. List the negative commands.

(2) Discuss some of the problems which are evident in our day when an individual Christian in his own home or the whole Christian church in the world neglects to follow verse 2 of this chapter.

CONCLUSION

Being a Christian involves every area of a person's life. Mind and body are yielded to God in moral surrender as a spiritual offering. By his attitudes and actions toward other Christians he is to demonstrate the fact that he is a fellow-member with them in the body of Christ. In his relationship with non-Christians, he is to act in love and to leave to God the avenging of evil.

Why Should a Christian Be in Subjection to Earthly Rulers?

This chapter deals with the Christian's relationships to earthly authorities, and to his neighbors, as well as the motivation for proper conduct.

Romans 13:1–7

(1) What reasons are given for submitting to civil authorities?

(2) How does this passage illustrate Paul's conviction about the sovereignty of God?

(3) What two things are stated about those who resist governmental powers?

(4) What is the function of government as stated in verses 3, 4? In what ways do all governments uphold the orderly life of society as God ordained?

(5) When and why should civil rulers be feared?

(6) In verses 6, 7, what illustrations are given of submission to civil authority? Compare with Mark 12:17. What qualification or limitation of this submission is suggested in both passages?

(7) In what way does a Christian's responsibility extend beyond paying his financial obligations to the government? What should we emphasize when teaching young people to show respect for officials of government, including law enforcement officials?

(8) Consider the historical background out of which Paul wrote these commands. (The Roman tyrant Nero ruled the empire at this time.) What help does this give us as we consider the Christian's responsibility toward his government, whether it is representative or totalitarian, in various societies of the world today?

Romans 13:8–14

(9) How does the Christian know what behavior is suitable in his relationships with others (verses 8–11)?

(10) How does the principle of love fulfill the laws mentioned in verse 9? How does love fulfill even civil laws such as traffic regulations?

(11) Chapter 12 began this section on practical Christian ethics with an appeal based on God's mercies revealed in Christ. On what truth does Paul base the appeal with which he concludes this section in verses 11–14?

(12) How does a Christian view time? Why is vigilance urged in regard to one's conduct?

(13) What emphasis is achieved by contrasting day and night, light and darkness?

(14) What three areas of wrongdoing are described in verse 13? Why is no difference in their seriousness implied?

(15) Discuss the meaning of each injuction in verses 12, 13, 14. Why is a negative and a positive suggested in each case? What does this indicate about the Christian life that is victorious over sin?

SUMMARY

How does the command in verse 14 provide the way for a Christian to fulfill his responsibilities to the government (verses 1–7)? to his neighbor (verses 8–10)? to God (verses 11–13)?

CONCLUSION

The commands of this chapter are as applicable to our generation as they were to Paul's day. The Christian should behave in every situation in accordance with *who God is* and *what God does*. The Christian's perspective is oriented to God's view of the world and God's purposes in the world. Christians essentially are spiritual revolutionaries, not political revolutionaries.

What About the Fact that Christians Differ in Their Opinions of Certain Practices?

The problem of how to handle the issues which divide one Christian from another is dealt with in this chapter. The weak Christian is defined.

Romans 14:1-12

(1) What particular difference of opinion among the Christians of Paul's time is suggested in verses 1-4?

(2) Who is characterized as the man weak in faith? Why?

(3) What warnings are given to those on both sides of the issue? What reasons are stated?

(4) What other example of a difference of opinion among Christians does Paul give?

(5) How does the ruling principle for Christian action (verse 6) cover Christians of both opinions?

(6) How is this thought developed in verses 7-12? On what motive and relationship is it essential that the Christian's choices be based?

(7) To whom is each Christian ultimately responsible (verses 10-12)? In this connection, how are the death and resurrection of Christ significant? How does this rule out criticism of our fellow Christians?

(8) Why is the admonition in verse 5b essential in the light of verse 12? What criterion has been suggested in this section as the basis for making decisions?

Romans 14:13-23

(9) Having addressed the strong and the weak together in the earlier part of the chapter, the apostle now gives additional advice to the "strong." What course are they urged to follow?

(10) In verses 13-21 consider the phrases by which Paul describes the "weak" one: a brother (13), your brother, one for whom Christ died (15), the work of God (20), your brother (21). What does he accomplish in this development of thought?

(11) Trace through this same section (verses 13–21) the possible effects wrought upon the weak one through the actions of the strong (i.e., tripped, hindered (verse 13), etc.).

(12) Compare verse 14 with verse 20. What are the important qualifying elements in these statements? When are certain actions unsuitable for a Christian? Remember that he is referring here to the types of questions dealt with in this chapter, not to moral issues clearly defined by commandments elsewhere in the Bible.

(13) What is the nature of the kingdom of God (verse 17)? In the light of this, what goals ought we to have? What specific things, do you think, are included in verse 19?

(14) In this chapter, what is the Christian's relationship to the different Persons of the Trinity?

(15) Love is to be the basis for our actions and reactions as far as other people are concerned. What do verses 22, 23 suggest as the basis for our attitudes and actions before God? Who is happy and who is condemned? Why?

SUMMARY

(1) State in your own words the basic principles given in this chapter concerning the proper action of Christians in situations where opinions differ as to what conduct is right.

(2) Give an illustration in our modern day life in which these principles apply.

CONCLUSION

Christian unity does not depend upon everyone conforming completely to a particular set of actions but upon conforming to the Lord Jesus in loving one another. Our freedom is conditioned by our love for the Lord and our love for one another.

Why Does Our Fellowship in Christ Transcend All Differences?

The early section of the chapter describes Christian social relationships, with Christ as the perfect example of them. Paul's personal message to the Romans begins in verse 14.

Romans 15: 1–13

(1) Put verse 1, 2 into your own words. Compare with 14:19.

(2) Why should the Christian practice such selflessness (verses 3, 4)? How will he be strengthened to do this (verses 4, 5)? What is the purpose or goal toward which Christians move (verses 5, 6)?

(3) How can the Scriptures be a source of practical encouragement for leading the Christian life? Read verse 4 in Phillips' translation. What is necessary on your part for the Scriptures to be helpful in your daily life?

(4) Compare verse 7 with 14:1 and 14:3. What thought is repeated? What is the standard of how we are to welcome or receive fellow Christians?

(5) What does verse 8a add to the thought expressed in verse 3a?

(6) What were the purposes of Christ's work (verses 7–9)? What peoples were affected?

(7) How do the Old Testament quotations in verses 9–12 substantiate the purpose for Christ's work stated in verse 9a?

(8) In chapters 14 and 15:1–3 Paul has been dealing with causes for divisions among Christians, divisions which can discourage and depress. Note the emphasis on hope in 15:4, 12, 13. What qualities are to characterize the Christian's life?

(9) Look quickly through verses 1–13 to discover all that is said concerning the identity and work of the Persons of the Trinity.

Romans 15:14–33

(10) What assurance does Paul have about the Christians at Rome? In what way does he exhibit tact?

(11) What would you know about Paul's work just from verses 15–21 if you had never read the book of Acts or any of

his letters beside this one? Consider what is revealed here about the nature of his job, his field of service, his goals, his methods, his area, his message, his ambitions.

(12) Why hasn't Paul visited the Christians at Rome before now? What situation has changed and what plans does Paul now have? What help does he expect from the Roman Christians?

(13) What is Paul's immediate task? Compare with Acts 19:21 and 24:17. Why and how are the Christians in Macedonia and Achaia concerned for the poor among the Christians at Jerusalem? What spiritual principle is Paul teaching the Romans by relating this news?

(14) What do verses 30–33 suggest about Paul? For what three things does he ask them to pray? From what you remember in your study of Acts, chapters 21–28, how were these three requests answered?

(15) What part does the Trinity play in Paul's thinking?

SUMMARY

(1) What is the nature and degree of the unity which is commanded for all who believe in the Lord Jesus Christ? Consider what this meant to the Jewish Christians and Gentile Christians in the early church. What are some contemporary equivalent situations?

(2) Read again verses 1, 2, 5, 6. Discuss practical examples from your own experience.

CONCLUSION

The motive and power behind Christian unity is Christ's example of love and service and sacrifice. To have such harmony among Christians we need to pray as Paul did for the Lord's enabling. Paul's sense of commission did not make him independent of his fellow Christians.

To What Sort of People Was This Letter Written?

Each name listed in Paul's closing remarks undoubtedly has a story of courage, love and devotion to the Lord Jesus Christ. Of the twenty-four to whom Paul sends special greetings, six are women, indicating the position and importance of women among the Christian groups at Rome.

Romans 16:1–16

(1) What do you learn about Phoebe who is to deliver this letter to Rome? What provisions does Paul make for her here? What example is set here as the standard for Christian hospitality?

(2) In verses 3–15 there is a list of some of those in Rome to whom Paul is writing. From the phrases describing them, what do you learn about the experiences, worship, and fellowship of these early Christians?

(3) Note the repetition of the phrases "in Christ" and "in the Lord." What do these phrases mean? What does this help you to understand about Paul's evaluation of people?

Romans 16:17–27

(4) What warning does Paul give in verses 17–20? At what point is the rule of Christian fellowship nullified? Why? Compare his exhortations in 15:1, 2, 7, and 14:1, 3 with his warning in 16:17 and in Galatians 1:7–9.

(5) What do you learn about Paul's companions from verses 21–23?

(6) In this benediction of praise to God for His power and wisdom (verses 25–27), Paul sums up his letter to the Romans. God strengthens the Christian according to (in agreement with, consistent with) what things?

(7) What was the "mystery kept secret for long ages" but now revealed from the Old Testament prophetic writings? See Ephesians 3:4–6; Romans 1:2–4; 3:21, 22.

(8) Sum up briefly what Paul has previously said in Romans about the inclusion of the Gentiles among the people of God.

SUMMARY

From this chapter, what impressions do you get of those to whom Paul is writing this letter?

CONCLUSION

Those who put their faith in Jesus Christ come into a fellowship of love, sharing, and responsibility with their fellow Christians.

* * * * *

REVIEW of Romans 1–16

What Is the Significance of the Doctrine Which This Letter Sets Forth?

(1) What are the main issues with which Paul deals in his letter to the Romans?

(2) How and why can a person obtain salvation? For whom is this salvation necessary? Why?

(3) What is the essence of the Christian life?

(4) What are some of the main points which Paul makes about the Jews?

(5) Describe some of the practical situations which are dealt with in this letter. Give illustrations of Christians in similar circumstances today.

(6) What qualities should characterize the mutual relationships of a group of Christians?

(7) Why is justification by faith the one way to God?

(8) Discuss what this letter teaches about the Lord Jesus Christ, about God the Father, and about the Holy Spirit.

Conclusion to the Study of Romans

Today many people believe that their goodness will get them to God. In contrast, J. B. Phillips in his comment on Romans says, "Salvation, i.e., being safe from the horrible long-term consequences of sin and safe in the presence of God's utter holiness, now becomes a matter of 'believing' and not 'achieving.' " Pride in the human heart caused the alienation of man from his Creator, and pride in the human heart is what keeps people today from accepting reconciliation with God according to His conditions. *These conditions,* as we have seen in Romans, *include* understanding our hopeless situation and accepting His free gift of life in Jesus Christ. This is justification by faith.

As long as you or I put confidence in ourselves and our own righteousness, we do not avail ourselves of the redemption purchased for us in the death of the Lord Jesus Christ. Each individual must ultimately make the decision to be either a self-trusting or a Christ-trusting person. Although the Christian life is a series of exercises in trusting Christ in all circumstances and events, a person *becomes* a Christian and receives God's free gift of salvation by making the initial decision to depend upon and obey Jesus as Savior and Lord.

This basic commitment in which you invite Jesus Christ into your heart and life to assume His rightful place as Sovereign Ruler may be made anywhere—at church, on the highway or at the kitchen sink. The important thing is not the outward setting, but the atmosphere of the heart. As the hymn writer puts it, "Let not conscience make you linger, nor of fitness fondly dream: all the fitness He requireth is to feel your need of Him."

Many say, "Well, I think I'm on the way" or "I've always believed these things" or "I don't know if I've ever really done this" or "I've said the words but nothing happened." To you the following suggestions may prove helpful:

1. Today make definite your commitment to the One who alone is able to give you the gift of salvation and eternal life.

Acknowledge your need of Jesus Christ as Savior and Lord.
Believe that His death was for your sake and in your place.
Commit yourself to Him and invite Him to enter and rule your life.

2. Begin to live out this commitment by recognizing in thought, word and deed that Jesus is in charge of your life.

3. Ask God to give you by His Holy Spirit the inner conviction and assurance that you now have a right standing with Him through His Son, Jesus Christ. Read I John 5: 9–13.

4. Share your experience with others, and enter into fellowship with those who also have this relationship to your Lord.

Bibliography

Barclay, William. *The Letter to the Romans* (Daily Study Bible).

Bruce, F. F. *The Epistle of Paul to the Romans* (Tyndale New Testament Commentaries.

Nee, Watchman. *The Normal Christian Life.*

Ross, Alexander. "The Pauline Epistles" in *The New Bible Commentary* edited by Francis Davidson, A. M. Stibbs and E. F. Kevan.

Stott, John R. W. *Men Made New* (An Exposition of Romans 5–8).

Thompson, G. T. and Davidson, F. "The Epistle to the Romans," in *The New Bible Commentary, Op. cit.*

BIBLE TRANSLATIONS
HELPFUL IN THE STUDY OF ROMANS:

Good News for Modern Man (The New Testament in Today's English Version).

Phillips, J. B. *The New Testament in Modern English.*

The New Testament (Revised Standard Version).

The Living New Testament, Paraphrased.

Williams, Charles B. *The New Testament in the Language of the People.*